The Story of the *Windrush*

K.N. Chimbiri

To Rafe + friends,
  I hope you all
enjoy this book about
the story of the Windrush.
With ~~warm~~ kind regards,
  K. N. Chimbiri

SCHOLASTIC

To my humble parents who like thousands of others of
the inspirational Windrush generation deserve thanks
for all they endured for us.

This edition published by Scholastic Children's Books, 2020
Euston House, 24 Eversholt Street, London, NW1 1DB

A division of Scholastic Limited
London ~ New York ~ Toronto ~ Sydney ~ Auckland
Mexico City ~ New Delhi ~ Hong Kong

First published in 2018 by Golden Destiny Ltd.

Text and illustrations © Kandace Chimbiri, 2020

ISBN 978 0702 30713 3

Printed and bound by Bell & Bain Ltd, UK

2 4 6 8 10 9 7 5 3

Contents

King Street, Kingston, Jamaica in the 1940s.

A Man Called Sam

In 1948, there was a young man called Sam King who lived in Jamaica, an island in the Caribbean. Sam was unhappy. The living conditions on the island were not good and there weren't many jobs available. Sam just wanted to leave.

Sam had left Jamaica before. He had travelled to England a few years earlier to help Britain during the Second World War. In those days, Jamaica was a British **colony**.* For hundreds of years, several European countries claimed colonies all over the world. Britain had the biggest **empire**.

*Words in **bold** are explained in the Glossary on page 44.

DOMINION OF CANADA
1763

New Foundland
1763

North
America

Bermuda Is.
1612

Gibraltar
1704

Bahama Is.
1648

Br. Honduras
1798

Jamaica
1655

Leeward Is.
1667

Afri

Barbados
1625

Gambia
1821

Windward Is.
1833

Trinidad
1797

Sierra
Leone
1787

Gold Coa
Colony
1871

Br. Guiana
1814

Western
Pacific
Islands
1877-1907

Ascension
1815

South
America

St Helena
1673

Tristan da Cunha
1816

Falkland Is.
1833

The British Empire, 1915. This map shows in red the lands ruled by Britain.

Europe

Asia

Tenedos
Lemnos
1915

Malta
1800

Cyprus
1878

Bahrain Is.
1867

North West
Frontier Province
1901

Baluchistan
1857

Sikkim
1890

Weihaiwei
1898

Egypt
1882

Hinderland
of Aden
1905

Perim
1857

Aden
1839

India
1858

Burma
1885

Kowloon
1860

Mainland of
Kowloon
1898

Hong Kong
1841

Sudan
1898

Socotra
1886

Somaliland
1887

Laccadive Is.
1892

Andaman Is.
1858

Ceylon
1796

Federated
Malay
States
1874

Br. North Borneo
1888

Uganda
1894

East Africa
Protectorate
1895

Nicobar Is.
1858

Penang
1786

Seychelles
1814

Zanzibar
Protectorate
1890

Malacca
1795

Singapore
1819

Br. N. Guinea
1884

Solomon Is.
1893

Western
Pacific Is.
1877–1907

Cocos Is.
1857

Rhodesia
1888–1923

echuana
Land
1885

Transvaal Prov.
1902

Mauritius
1810

Zululand
1887

Fiji Is.
1874

Good
Prov.

Orange Free State Prov.
1806

Basutoland
1871

Natal Prov.
1843

Commonwealth
of Australia

1788

Tasmania
1803

New Zealand
1840

The dates show roughly when they became a part of the empire.

A classroom in Jamaica in the 1940s.

CHAPTER ONE
The Second World War

Many of the people who lived in these British colonies believed that England was their **'mother country'**. Some of Britain's colonies were in the Caribbean, which was made up of **first people** as well as people from Europe, Africa, Asia and the Middle East. Most people in the Caribbean were of African descent; however, in school the students were taught little about Africa or the Caribbean. Instead, the focus was on England and English history.

Because of their loyalty to the 'mother country', when Britain declared war on Germany in 1939, people in the British colonies wanted to help Britain. Sam's mother said to him, 'My son, the Mother Country's at war. Go and help. If you live, it will be a good thing'.

Sam applied for a job with the Royal Air Force (RAF) in England. He passed the tests and initial training in Jamaica, then travelled to England with other volunteers. After three more months of training, Sam worked for the RAF in England as an engineer.

Around a thousand Royal Air Force volunteers from the Caribbean arriving in Liverpool, England in June 1944.

Sam was just one of many men and women from all over the world who came to help Britain during the Second World War. However, after the war ended, the British government wouldn't

let Sam stay in Britain. He didn't want to go back to Jamaica but he had no choice.

RAF Pilot Officer Ulric Leslie Look Yan came from Trinidad in 1943 to help Britain.

CHAPTER TWO
A New Opportunity

A few months after returning to Jamaica, Sam
saw an advertisement in a Jamaican newspaper:

Passenger Opportunity
To United Kingdom

Troopship 'EMPIRE WINDRUSH' sailing
about 23rd MAY.
Fares: – Cabin Class.................**£48**
Troopdeck.............................**£28**
Royal Mail Lines, Limited – 8 Port Royal St.

The *Daily Gleaner*. Thursday, 15 April 1948.

This was Sam's chance to return to England!
The ship's fare of twenty-eight pounds (£28)
was not cheap. For some people this was three
months' **salary**. Sam came from a family of
farmers; they sold three of their cows to raise
the money for his fare.

Sam was one of more than 500 passengers who boarded the HMT *Empire Windrush* in Jamaica. However, Sam and the other Jamaicans were not the first Caribbean people on board the *Windrush*. The ship had already stopped at another British colony called Trinidad. Many Trinidadians also believed that England was their 'mother country' and they too wanted to go to Britain.

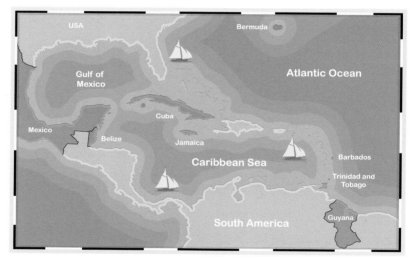

The Caribbean region today. Trinidad is near the South American mainland.

Peter Dielhenn

Peter Dielhenn, an Englishman who worked in the ship's bakery, was surprised to see hundreds of **civilians**, many of African descent, boarding the ship to go to England. He was one of the 240 **crew** who worked on the *Windrush*. When the *Windrush* first sailed from England earlier that year it had about 2,000 passengers on board: mostly White men, nearly all soldiers from England, Scotland and Ireland. The *Windrush* was a **troopship**, carrying British soldiers to and from the colonies throughout the world. Peter thought that the ship would return to England empty apart from its crew; he didn't know that the ship would be picking up non-military passengers on the way back. 'It was really something to see,' he later recalled.

The *Windrush* also stopped to pick up passengers at Tampico in Mexico and also Bermuda before departing for England.

Some of the Caribbean people on board the *Windrush* were of Indian descent.

At Tampico, 66 Polish people, nearly all women and children, joined the ship. During the war, they had left Poland and ended up in Mexico for their safety. Now, they too were coming to England.

On board the *Windrush* were more than a thousand passengers from the Caribbean, Britain, Bermuda, Poland, Gibraltar and Burma. However, it was the Caribbean people who made up the majority of the ship's passengers.

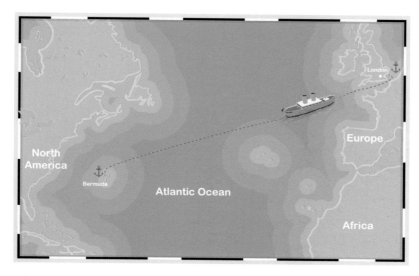

This map shows the last stage of HMT *Empire Windrush*'s journey from Bermuda to Britain.

Some passengers felt unwell due to the motion of the ship, the English food served on board or the weather.

CHAPTER THREE
The Voyage

Peter Dielhenn remembered the voyage as
a 'quite jolly occasion'. He thought that the
Caribbean people were very 'lively'. Some of
the passengers did enjoy their journey from the
Caribbean to England. Others hated it.

Alford Gardner from Jamaica was delighted to
find that there were Trinidadians, **Barbadians**
and other Caribbean nationalities on board. He
found it was very easy to make friends with the
other Caribbean people. He recalled, 'All you
had to do was mingle.'

Some of the Trinidadians on the ship were
musicians who played **calypso** music. Calypso
is an African-Caribbean style of music which
originated in Trinidad and Tobago. Three of the
Trinidadian **calypsonians** who had boarded the
Windrush were famous male singers called Lord
Kitchener, Lord Woodbine and Lord Beginner.
On the ship, Lord Kitchener began to write a

song called 'London is the Place for Me', which would later become famous.

While some of the Caribbean people on the *Windrush* had already arranged jobs in Britain, others were in the same position as Sam; they hoped to find a job when they arrived. Arthur Leigh had no money and no job, but he decided to go anyway because, 'It was an opportunity.'

George McPherson spent some of the trip working. He got a job in the ship's bakery so that he would have a bit more money when he arrived in England. He fondly remembered the journey: 'We had a fabulous time.'

One day George was working in the bakery, when he heard a noise. He looked around and was shocked to find a woman in hiding. George had found a **stowaway**! She wanted to come to England too but she didn't have enough money for the fare. So, she had sneaked on board and hidden herself. And now she was hungry! Many of the other passengers felt sorry for her. So, they had a 'whip round' – passengers put

Calypso music and shows like this one came to
Britain before the *Windrush*.

together some of their own money until they collected enough to pay the fare on her behalf. Now she too could legally travel to England.

Many of the Caribbean people on the *Windrush* had never been to Britain before, so Sam and the others who had been to Britain during the war told them what to expect. They explained that the country was in a bad way, the war had left London poor and scruffy, food was rationed, and the cities were bombed out. But the important thing was that there were lots of jobs available.

This undated photo shows office workers as they go to work after a heavy bombing raid on London during the Second World War.

Although most of the Caribbean passengers on the *Windrush* were men, many women and children came, too. Mona Baptiste, a young Trinidadian, was one of the many Caribbean women who came to Britain on the *Windrush*.

This photo shows Mona Baptiste, a famous singer and musician from Trinidad. The *Daily Gleaner* newspaper in Jamaica reported on the front page that she was travelling to England on board the *Windrush*.

Lord Kitchener sings 'London is the Place for Me' for the media.

CHAPTER FOUR
Starting a New Life

On 21 June 1948, the *Windrush* arrived at Tilbury Docks in Essex. The following day, when the new arrivals began to disembark, the media was there. Lord Kitchener, the Trinidadian calypsonian, sang the first part of his new song, 'London Is The Place For Me' for the news cameras.

Those, who like Sam did not already have jobs, were taken in minibuses to Clapham in south-west London. There, they were housed in a collection of underground tunnels called Clapham South deep-level shelter, which had been an air-raid shelter some years ago. Local people had hidden there at night for safety from the German bombs during the Second World War.

Children in the Clapham South deep-level shelter in 1944, during the Second World War.

Sam and his friends did not always receive a warm welcome. Although Britain was still reeling from the after-effects of the war and there were lots of jobs related to the rebuilding of the country, many British people did not want to give jobs to Black people.

In colonial times some British people travelled to the colonies as **settlers**, soldiers or workers. However, p eople from the colonies, especially those were not white, were not expected to come to Britain.

Windrush arrivals, who did not yet have jobs, queueing at a job centre inside Clapham South deep-level shelter, 1948.

Finding good jobs was also not easy for the *Windrush* passengers. Sometimes the new arrivals were paid less than White workers for the same job. Others often had to accept **menial** or low-paid jobs. Despite this, they didn't give up and after a month all the *Windrush* arrivals had a job. Some, like Sam, found work again with the RAF. Others found work with the new National Health Service (NHS). Most found jobs in London, but some moved to other parts of Britain.

The Windrush passengers at Clapham South deep-level shelter slept in tunnels beneath the underground train lines.

CHAPTER FIVE
Settling Down

Another big challenge for the *Windrush* arrivals was finding a place to live. Once they had found jobs, they had to leave Clapham South deep-level shelter. But many White people didn't want to rent rooms to Black people.

When Mr and Mrs Holness saw an advertisement for a room to rent in Tooting, south London, Mr Holness phoned in advance to inform the landlady that he wasn't English. But when he arrived he was refused the room. The landlady didn't mind renting the room to a foreigner but she didn't want to rent to a Black foreigner.

Many of the *Windrush* newcomers had a similar experience. It wasn't because they didn't have the money to pay the rent or because of anything they had done. They were refused somewhere to live simply because they were Black.

Not everyone who had sailed on the *Windrush* planned to stay in Britain permanently. Some people just wanted to work hard, make money and then return to the Caribbean when the living conditions there improved. Those who did end up staying, came together to develop their own community. They formed their own churches as they were often made to feel unwelcome in the White British Christian churches. Others used an African–Caribbean savings method to help each other so they

 didn't need to go to banks for money. Some managed to buy their own houses, and would then rent spare rooms to other Caribbean people.

Lord Kitchener eventually decided to return to Trinidad.

Landladies, like this one, often refused to rent rooms to Black people.

Allan served with the Royal Navy and RAF during the war.

CHAPTER SIX
Before the *Windrush*

The *Windrush* was not the first ship to bring Caribbean people to Britain after the war.

In March 1947, the SS *Ormonde* brought more than 100 Caribbean immigrants to Liverpool. Then, in December 1947, six months before the arrival of the *Windrush*, the SS *Almanzora* brought around 200 Caribbean **immigrants** to Southampton. One of those on board was a young man called Allan Wilmot.

Allan came from a well-off family in Jamaica. Many of the Caribbean people who came before, and later, on the *Windrush* were well-educated, talented people.

Allan, like Sam, had served Britain during the Second World War. Now he was returning during peacetime but things were different. People said to him, 'The war is over. What are you doing here?' He ended up, for a time, hungry, homeless and without a job.

Allan's father was a merchant ship's captain and the family were well-off.

CHAPTER SEVEN
The Windrush Generation

Between 1947 and 1971 at least 300,000 people from the Caribbean came to Britain. These people are called the 'Windrush generation', although they didn't all arrive on the *Windrush* ship. They are the **foreparents** of many of today's Black British people.

The Windrush generation came to Britain for many reasons. Some people were invited to Britain to work. Both the NHS and London Transport asked Caribbean people to come to Britain to work for them. Other people found jobs after they came to Britain. Many people wanted to work and send some money back to the Caribbean to help their families there. Some people wanted to come to Britain mainly to study.

During these years, many of the Windrush generation continued to face hardship and poor treatment from some of the White British population. Sometimes they were even physically attacked.

Yet the Windrush generation continued to work hard and raise their children. They worked for the RAF, London Transport, Royal Mail and the National Health Service. They also worked in Britain's coal mines, on the railways, in entertainment and in many other industries.

Caribbean people arriving in Britain on 24 October 1952.

These brave **pioneers** helped to rebuild Britain after the Second World War and make it into today's modern nation. They helped the **economy** by doing a variety of jobs. They also added to Britain's culture through food, dance, music, art and writing. But most of all, they made people talk more about how we should treat others from different backgrounds. And now, people from all over the world have emigrated to Britain. By striving to improve their own lives, the Windrush pioneers changed the world.

People in Bridgetown, Barbados in 1948 waiting for a ship to take them to Britain.

Two recruitment officers from London Transport interviewing
Caribbean men for jobs in Britain, in Barbados in 1956.

An African-Caribbean man working on a steam locomotive on 17
May 1962.

Two Caribbean men reading the room 'To Let' accommodation notices in a shop window, Notting Hill Gate, London, in 1955.

Sam B. King, MBE (1926–2016)

CHAPTER EIGHT
Keeping the Story Alive

After rejoining the RAF, Sam later worked for the postal service, Royal Mail. Then he went into politics and in 1983 he became the first Black mayor of the London Borough of Southwark. With his friend Arthur Torrington from Guyana, Sam also set up a charity called the Windrush Foundation to help keep alive the real story of the *Windrush*.

RAF officers recruiting new arrivals on board the *Windrush* on 22 June 1948. Sam can be seen at the back of the group, on the right.

The Story of the Windrush: **Timeline**

- **1939:** Start of the Second World War. People from the colonies help Britain to win the war.

- **1945:** End of the Second World War. Britain is left devastated and needs people to help rebuild the country.

- **1947:** Two ships, the SS *Ormonde* and the SS *Almanzora*, arrive in England with hundreds of Caribbean people on board.

- **1948:** The British Nationality Act is passed by the British government. It confirms that people from all of Britain's colonies can come and settle in Britain. In June, the HMT *Empire Windrush* arrives at Tilbury Docks, Essex with hundreds of Caribbean men, women and children on board.

- **1949:** The National Health Service (NHS) asks people from the Caribbean to come to Britain and work for them.

- **1956:** London Transport recruits people from the Caribbean to come to Britain and work for them.

- **1958:** Violence and discrimination against Black people leads to race **riots** in places like Notting Hill in London and in Nottingham.

- **1959:** Trinidadian journalist Claudia Jones organizes the first indoor Caribbean carnival in a peaceful response to the race riots.

- **1962:** Commonwealth Immigrants Act limits immigration from Britain's colonies.

- **1965:** Race Relations Act is passed to address racial discrimination for the first time.

- **1971:** The Immigration Act is passed. Large-scale Caribbean immigration to Britain ends.

- **2018:** The first annual Windrush Day is held, a national day to celebrate the Windrush generation and their descendants.

Glossary

This glossary explains some of the words you have come across when reading about the *Windrush*.

Barbadian A person from the island of Barbados.

Calypso An African–Caribbean style of music that originated in Trinidad and Tobago.

Calypsonian A singer of calypso.

Civilian A person who is not in the armed forces.

Colony A country or geographical area that is ruled in some way by another country. See also Empire and Mother country.

Crew The group of people who manage, operate and serve on a ship.

Discrimination Unfair treatment of a person or group of people because of where they come from, what they look like or other personal traits. Discrimination because of race is called racism.

Economy The system of how money is made and used in a country.

Empire A group of lands or colonies under the control of one powerful person, country or government.

First people The earliest people known to live in a particular area that is then taken over by another group of people.

Foreparents Members of past generations of a family.

Immigrant A person who comes to a new country in order to live there permanently. See also Settlers.

Menial Work that is unskilled and often of low status.

Mother country The homeland of the colonizers. See also Colony.

Pioneer A person who is the first to start something new so others can follow.

Riot Violent and uncontrolled public behaviour by a large number of people.

Salary A regular payment made by an employer to an employee in return for their work.

Settlers People who move away from their homeland to live permanently in a new country.

Stowaway A person who hides on a ship, aircraft or other vehicle to avoid paying the fare.

Troopship A ship that transports soldiers in wartime or in peacetime.

Useful resources for parents, teachers and educators

Books:

Robin Walker, Vanika Marshall, Paula Perry and Anthony Vaughan, *Black British History: Black Influences on British Culture* (1948 to 2016) (2017)

Allan Wilmot, *Now You Know: The Memoirs of Allan Charles Wilmot* (2015)

Organizations:

The Windrush Foundation   windrushfoundation.com

Black Cultural Archives   blackculturalarchives.org

Black History Walks   blackhistorywalks.co.uk

Credits

Illustrations by Corne-Enroc.

Book design and layout by Valeria Maria Mazzitelli.

Maps on pages 14 and 17 by Vaclav Bicha.

Map of the British Empire in 1915 on pages 6 & 7 by Anis Yusha.

Quotations on pages 9, 15, 19 and 20 are taken from the Windrush Pioneers booklet and DVD produced by the Windrush Foundation's Oral History Project.

Quotation on page 33 is from Allan Wilmot's autobiography *Now You Know: The Memoirs of Allan Charles Wilmot*.

Picture Credits (in page order)

THE SECOND WORLD WAR

10 ©Imperial War Museum (CH 13438)
12 ©Imperial War Museum (D 15031)

THE VOYAGE

22 ©Imperial War Museum (HU 36157)
23 Trinity Mirror / Mirrorpix / Alamy Stock Photo

STARTING A NEW LIFE

26 Image supplied by London Transport Museum
27 Credit ©TopFoto

THE WINDRUSH GENERATION

36 © Daily Herald Archive/National Science & Media Museum / Science
& Society Picture Library
37 Image supplied by London Transport Museum
38 (Top) ©TfL from the London Transport Museum collection
38 (Bottom) Credit © Colin T Gifford / Science & Society Picture Library
39 Image supplied by London Transport Museum

KEEPING THE STORY ALIVE

41 Credit ©TopFoto

Every effort has been made to trace and acknowledge ownership
of copyright. If any rights have been omitted, the publishers offer to
rectify this in any future editions following notification

Acknowledgements

The author would very much like to thank Tony Warner and
Darren Chetty for reading the draft and offering detailed feedback.
Their suggestions and advice resulted in a much improved text.
Thanks also to Robin Walker for a useful discussion on the number
of passengers onboard the Windrush.

Thanks also to friends and family who offered support,
encouragement and feedback: Amanda, Angel, Auntie Rose, Dee,
Deborah, Diana and Jay.

Index

Words in **bold** can be found in the Glossary. Numbers refer to pages.
Numbers in italics (e.g. *24*) are page numbers for pictures or photos.